Muffins
and turnips

Mum is off to the market.

She has been cooking
muffins to sell. She will
sell hot coffee too.

Miss Good is keen to
go with Mum. She has
turnips she wishes to sell.

Mum picks Miss Good up.
She gets into the van with
her box of turnips.

Sid curls up on a rug by
Mum and is purring.

Miss Good pats Sid's fur and tells him he is such a good dog.

Mum thinks that is a bit odd. She looks at Miss Good to see if she has her specs on.

No specs, Miss Good?

Then Miss Good tells Mum,
"Look out for that goat on
the road."

Mum can see a
bin, but no goat.

At the market Mum sets up her coffee urn, cups and muffins.

Miss Good sets up her turnips.

Mum sits a muffin on
a napkin for Miss Good.

Then Mum looks back at
the urn to turn it on. Miss
Good picks up her muffin.

Words to blend

market	cooking	Good
looks	coffee	keen
see	wishes	with
such	missing	goat
road	right	thing
think	that	then
napkin	muffin	picks

Before reading

Synopsis: Mum is going to the market to sell muffins and coffee. Miss Good comes with her to sell her turnips but her specs are missing – again!

Review graphemes/phonemes: ar or

New grapheme/phoneme: ur

Story discussion: Look at the cover and read the title together. Ask: *Which characters are in this story?* (Mum and Miss Good) *What do you think they're doing?* (getting ready to sell muffins and turnips)

Link to prior learning: Display the grapheme *ur*. Say: *These two letters are a digraph, that means they make one sound.* Write or display these words: *hurt, burn, surf, curl.* How quickly can children identify the *ur* grapheme and read the words?

Vocabulary check: urn – a container for hot drinks

Decoding practice: Display these words: *market, turnip, burn, form, sort, part, morning, surf, car, fur, north.* How quickly can children read the words and sort them into groups according to whether they have *ar, or, ur*?

Tricky word practice: Display the word *out* and ask children to circle the tricky part of the word (*ou*, which makes an /ow/ sound). Practise writing and reading this word.

After reading

Apply learning: Ask: *Do you think it was kind of Mum to say that Miss Good was right about the muffin, at the end of the story? Why do you think she did that?* (e.g. Perhaps so that Miss Good wouldn't feel bad about her mistake.)

Comprehension

- Why does Miss Good not have her specs?

- What is Mum going to sell at the market? What is Miss Good going to sell?

- Why does Miss Good think Mum's muffin is "a bit odd"?

Fluency

- Pick a page that most of the group read quite easily. Ask them to reread it with pace and expression. Model how to do this if necessary.

- Ask children to turn to pages 8–9 and read the speech bubbles with lots of expression.

- Practise reading the words on page 17.

Tricky words review

and	to	the
she	go	into
her	by	no
out	you	my
for	your	are